SPORTS IN THE NEWS

PRO ATHLETE PAY EQUITY

by Martha London

FOCUS READERS®

VOYAGER

www.focusreaders.com

Focus Readers is distributed by North Star Editions:
sales@northstareditions.com | 888-417-0195

Produced for Focus Readers by Red Line Editorial.

Photographs ©: Francisco Seco/AP Images, cover, 1; Matthias Schrader/AP Images, 4–5 (top); Shutterstock Images, 4–5 (bottom), 41; Mark J. Terrill/AP Images, 7, 19; John Rooney/AP Images, 8–9, 22–23; AP Images, 11, 21; Red Line Editorial, 13, 25; Nick Ut/AP Images, 14–15; Robin Trimarchi/KRT/Newscom, 17; Mark Humphrey/AP Images, 27; Patrick Semansky/AP Images, 28–29, 42–43; Ross D. Franklin/AP Images, 31; Zsolt Szigetvary/MTI/AP Images, 33; Matt Dunbar/World Surf League/Getty Images, 35; Nick Wass/AP Images, 36–37; Tony Avelar/AP Images, 39; John Crouch/Icon Sportswire, 45

Library of Congress Cataloging-in-Publication Data
Names: London, Martha, author.
Title: Pro athlete pay equity / Martha London.
Description: Lake Elmo, MN : Focus Readers, 2021. | Series: Sports in the news | Includes index. | Audience: Grades 4-6
Identifiers: LCCN 2020004012 (print) | LCCN 2020004013 (ebook) | ISBN 9781644933923 (Hardcover) | ISBN 9781644934685 (Paperback) | ISBN 9781644936207 (PDF) | ISBN 9781644935446 (eBook)
Subjects: LCSH: Professional sports--Economic aspects. | Sports for women--Economic aspects. | Professional sports--Social aspects. | Sports for women--Social aspects. | Sex discrimination in sports. | Discrimination in sports. | Mass media and sports--Social aspects.
Classification: LCC GV716 .L65 2021 (print) | LCC GV716 (ebook) | DDC 796.06/91--dc23
LC record available at https://lccn.loc.gov/2020004012
LC ebook record available at https://lccn.loc.gov/2020004013

Printed in the United States of America
Mankato, MN
082020

ABOUT THE AUTHOR

Martha London lives and works in Minnesota. She writes books for young readers full-time. When Martha isn't writing, you can find her hiking in the woods.

TABLE OF CONTENTS

CHAPTER 1

PAY GAP

Professional athletes are members of an elite group. They get paid to play the sports they love. To compete at such a high level, pro athletes must practice for hours every day. But at the end of their workouts, male and female athletes go home to very different realities.

Male athletes tend to earn very high salaries. They often get big **endorsement** deals, too. As a result, men can earn millions of dollars per year.

The French men's team received $38 million for winning the World Cup. The US women's team got $4 million for winning the Women's World Cup.

In contrast, female athletes in the same sports earn much smaller salaries. Women also get fewer endorsement deals. And when they do get deals, they tend to be much smaller than men's.

Some people argue that this pay gap exists because fewer fans watch women's sports. Due to lower viewership, women's leagues bring in less money. For this reason, critics of equal pay say women simply can't receive the same amount as men.

However, many **advocates** are working to close the gender pay gap in sports. Their goal is to eventually have equal pay for male and female

> **THINK ABOUT IT**

Other than pro sports, what are some other examples of men and women being paid differently for the same work?

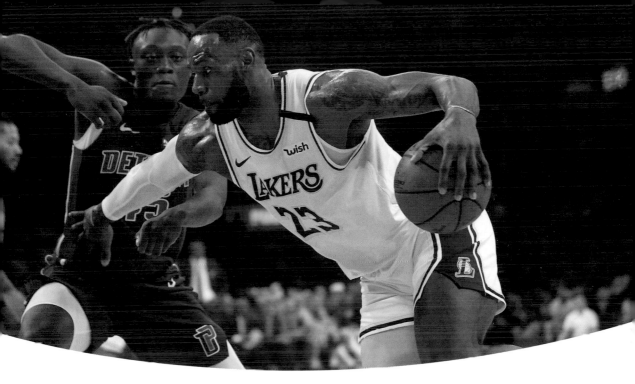

▲ During the 2019–20 basketball season, LeBron James earned $55 million from endorsements.

athletes. One step on that path is achieving fair pay. This means female athletes can earn salaries that reflect their talents.

Fair pay allows female athletes to fully participate in their sports. As it stands, that's not always the case. The current pay gap between male and female athletes is so extreme that some women have left their sports entirely.

CHAPTER 2

HISTORY OF PRO ATHLETE PAY

In the early 1900s, nearly all pro athletes were men. Women had limited opportunities to play sports. Many doctors incorrectly believed sports were bad for women's health. Other people thought it was inappropriate for women to take part in competitive games.

Even for male athletes, pay has not always been equal. Until the late 1940s, professional sports in the United States were **segregated** by race.

For decades, black players such as Jackie Robinson earned less than white players.

For example, Major League Baseball (MLB) had racist policies that prevented black players from entering the league. Instead, black athletes had to play in the Negro Leagues. They could not earn as much money in those leagues.

In 1947, an MLB team finally signed a black player. Jackie Robinson joined the Brooklyn Dodgers. He spent 10 seasons in the majors, and he was one of the game's best players. Even so, Robinson earned less than half of what the top white players made.

In the 1950s and 1960s, women had new opportunities to play professional sports. Most of these opportunities were limited to individual sports, such as golf and tennis. Female golfers and tennis players earned far less than men. And team sports still weren't an option for women who wanted to play professionally.

In the 1950s, Althea Gibson won Wimbledon twice.

Male athletes' earnings began to rise in the 1960s. Television played a big role in this trend. TV stations started paying leagues huge amounts of money for the rights to show their games. Some of this money went back to the players.

By the 1990s, hundreds of male athletes were earning more than $1 million per year. From there, salaries continued to climb. In the 2000s, several male athletes signed multi-year contracts worth $20 million or more each year. By this time, race was no longer a major factor in how much athletes could earn. However, gender still had a huge effect on salaries.

Investment in women's sports was much lower than for men's sports. For this reason, women's sports grew more slowly. By the late 2010s, there were pro women's leagues in basketball, hockey, soccer, and softball. But they had few endorsements. Many of these leagues struggled to get their games shown on TV. As a result, they didn't make much money. That meant they had to keep costs down. One of these costs was player salaries. Most players didn't earn anywhere close to $1 million per year.

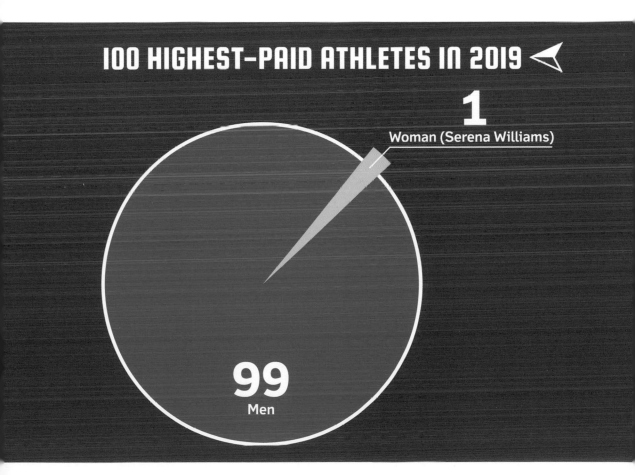

100 HIGHEST-PAID ATHLETES IN 2019

1
Woman (Serena Williams)

99
Men

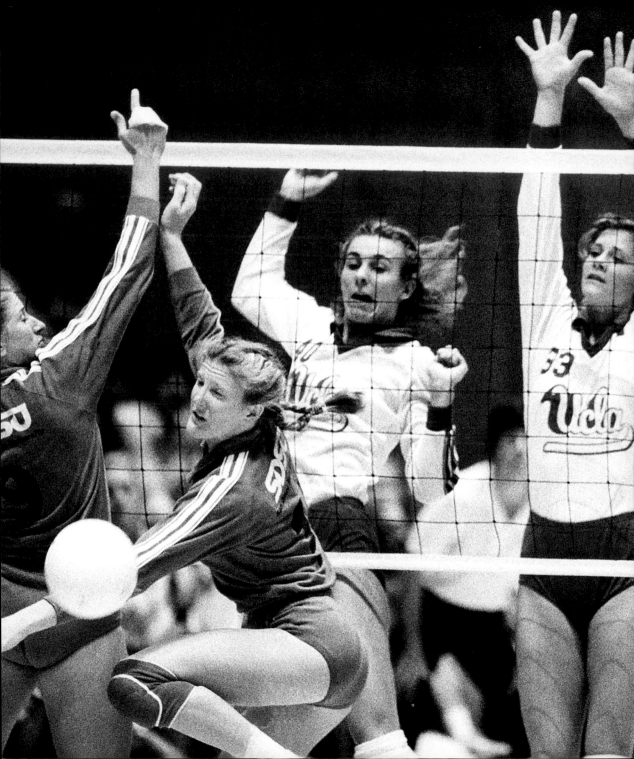

CHAPTER 3

FIGHTING FOR OPPORTUNITY

Laws dealing with athletic participation have changed over time. In the United States, one of the biggest changes was the passage of Title IX. This law look effect in 1972. Title IX guaranteed equal opportunities for boys and girls in schools. These opportunities included school sports.

Before the passage of Title IX, only 1 percent of all sports funding went to women's teams. And only 4 percent of school-age girls played sports.

Title IX enabled many female athletes to take part in college sports.

By the late 2010s, approximately 40 percent of girls played sports. Title IX had opened the door for more participation in college sports. From there, the next step was to create opportunities for the top female athletes who had finished school. But professional women's sports leagues took years to form.

By the mid-1990s, women's sports had more **commercial** success than ever before. In particular, the 1996 Olympics and 1999 Women's World Cup signaled potential turning points for female athletes.

At the 1996 Olympics, women made huge strides. The US women's teams won gold in soccer, softball, basketball, and gymnastics. But these milestones were not the only feats that female athletes achieved. Women also had more marketing opportunities than in the past.

▲ Team USA softball player Kim Maher slides into home during the 1996 Olympics.

For example, female athletes **promoted** shoes and sports equipment. Women also appeared in several TV ads. As a result, more people began to recognize women as athletes and Olympians.

In addition, the media began giving women's sports more coverage. News reports discussed women's sports in a similar way to men's sports.

This coverage led to further strides in women's sports. The Women's National Basketball Association (WNBA) began its first season in 1997. Two years later, women's soccer took the United States by storm. The US Women's National Team (USWNT) won the 1999 Women's World Cup in a thrilling shootout on home soil.

The USWNT has continued to be extremely successful over the years. In contrast, the men's team has seen much less success. Even so, the men's players earned more money from the US Soccer Federation. Critics of equal pay argued that the men are paid more because men's soccer

> **THINK ABOUT IT**

In your opinion, how does the media influence the way people think about women's sports?

⬆ Brandi Chastain scores the winning goal of the 1999 Women's World Cup.

brings in more money. But supporters of the women's team pointed out that players on both teams performed the same job. Because of that, they believe players on both teams should be paid equally. In 2019, the USWNT sued US Soccer for **discrimination**. Players felt their success on the field should be rewarded fairly. The lawsuit was scheduled to go to court in 2020.

BATTLE OF THE SEXES

In 1973, more than 90 million people turned on their TVs to watch a tennis match. Bobby Riggs was taking on Billie Jean King. Riggs was a former No. 1 player in men's tennis. He claimed women were not as good at tennis as men. At 55 years old, Riggs said he could easily beat any woman. He challenged King to a match.

At the time, King was 29 years old. She was a leader in pushing for equal rights for women. And she was determined to prove Riggs wrong.

King beat Riggs in three straight sets. But even after her victory, some people made excuses for Riggs. For example, announcers said King hit many short shots that Riggs could not get to. They believed Riggs would have beaten King if he had been younger.

Despite these critics, King knew her victory was important for female tennis players around the

⏶ Billie Jean King prepares to serve during her 1973 match against Bobby Riggs.

world. Beating Riggs was not the point. Instead, the point was introducing women's tennis to more people. King showed 90 million people that women were just as exciting to watch as men.

CHAPTER 4

RECENT EVENTS IN PRO ATHLETE PAY

The four biggest tournaments in tennis are known as the Grand Slams. Thousands of people attend these matches. Millions more watch them on TV. But for years, men's prize money was much higher than women's. Tennis legend Billie Jean King worked to change that. In 1973, her efforts helped convince the US Open to offer equal prize money. However, the other Grand Slams continued to pay men more.

Margaret Court received $25,000 for winning the women's singles title at the 1973 US Open. The men's winner received the same amount.

In 2005, Venus Williams fought for equity at Wimbledon and the French Open. At that time, the French Open and Wimbledon were the last two Grand Slam tournaments that did not offer equal pay. Soon after Williams spoke out, the French Open gave men and women the same pay. Wimbledon began offering pay equity in 2007. However, the four Grand Slam tournaments are not the norm. As of 2020, most smaller tennis tournaments still didn't offer equal pay.

Women's team sports have also made gains in recent years. In 2016, a softball player signed the sport's first million-dollar contract. Monica Abbott was a pitcher for the Scrap Yard Dawgs in Houston, Texas. Before that, Abbott won an Olympic silver medal with Team USA. Abbott and the National Pro Fastpitch (NPF) league saw the contract as a huge milestone. It was the first million-dollar contract offered to a female athlete. Advocates hoped Abbott's contract would open the door to higher pay for professional female athletes in all sports.

Asking for better pay does not always work. Sometimes players have to protest. In 2017, players on the Women's US National Hockey Team threatened to **boycott** the Women's World Championships. The players wanted fairer pay.

WIMBLEDON SINGLES PRIZE MONEY

Year	Men	Women
1968	£2,000	£750
1974	£10,000	£7,000
1980	£20,000	£18,000
1986	£140,000	£126,000
1992	£265,000	£240,000
1998	£435,000	£391,500
2004	£602,500	£560,500
2010	£1,000,000	£1,000,000
2016	£2,000,000	£2,000,000
2018	£2,250,000	£2,250,000

They also wanted multi-year contracts. The boycott was a risky move. League officials could have chosen not to meet with them.

In March 2017, many players felt negotiations were not getting anywhere. But eventually, the boycott worked. USA Hockey and the players agreed to a four-year contract. However, that didn't solve everything. Their professional league still faced many challenges. Players earned very little money in the National Women's Hockey League (NWHL). And NWHL teams offered only one-year contracts. That meant players had very little stability. The players wanted better.

> ## THINK ABOUT IT

How might a multi-year contract help promote pay equality for professional female athletes?

▲ NWHL players compete in the league's 2019 All-Star Game.

Despite the agreement with USA Hockey, players continued to feel neglected by the NWHL.

In 2019, more than 200 players agreed not to play in the league. The players hoped the National Hockey League (NHL) would step in. Players in the NWHL wanted a single league run by the NHL. This league would oversee both men's and women's hockey. They hoped a single league would lead to better pay.

CHAPTER 5

MAKING ENDS MEET

Professional basketball is one of the most well-known examples of unequal pay. In 2019, the maximum salary for a WNBA player was $117,500. However, players could also earn bonuses. So, the most a WNBA player could make was approximately $200,000. That same year, the NBA's highest-paid player earned more than $40 million. And the NBA's minimum salary was nearly $900,000.

WNBA star Elena Delle Donne earned a base salary of $115,000 in 2019. Even the referees in the NBA earned more.

Some WNBA players struggle to make ends meet on their low salaries. For this reason, players often take on extra work. Many compete in winter leagues in other countries. However, playing two separate seasons each year causes wear and tear on an athlete's body. NBA players, meanwhile, make far more money while also having more time to rest.

In 2015, Diana Taurasi sat out the entire WNBA season. She was in good health. But her team in Russia paid her a bonus to not play in the United States. The bonus was higher than her entire WNBA salary. Taurasi decided to take the money.

It wasn't just the pay that convinced Taurasi. She wanted to make a point. She could earn more money not playing than she could playing. Many fair-pay advocates began asking questions about the WNBA. They wondered if it was reasonable

▲ Diana Taurasi is the WNBA's all-time scoring leader.

for players to compete year-round just to earn a decent living.

In early 2019, Breanna Stewart suffered a bad leg injury during her overseas season. The injury forced her to miss the entire 2019 WNBA season.

Stewart had been the WNBA's MVP in 2018. But her injury kept her from playing again. Fair-pay advocates hoped this event would be a turning point for the WNBA.

Indeed it was. In 2020, WNBA players reached a new agreement with the league. Under the new deal, the maximum salary nearly doubled. Players can now earn up to $215,000 in base salary. And with bonuses, they can earn more than $500,000. The minimum salary also increased from $42,000 to $57,000. Thanks to these pay increases, many players will no longer choose to go overseas to earn extra money.

In addition, the new deal gave players better travel arrangements. Previously, players sat in the airplane's main cabin. Now, they sit in premium seats that offer more leg room. Also, many players used to be required to share hotel rooms. Now,

▲ Brittney Griner plays for Russian team
UMMC Ekaterinburg in 2018.

each player gets her own room. Players said
these benefits would help them get more rest.
They believed their performance in games would
improve as a result.

SURFING TOWARD EQUALITY

In 2016, six female surfers came together to create a new foundation. They called it the **Commission** for Equity in Women's Surfing (CEWS). Its goal is making sure men and women receive equal prize money.

The world's best surfers compete in the World Surf League (WSL). In 2018, the WSL announced equal pay for all surfers in its Championship Tour series. But leaders of CEWS say their work is not done. Pay inequality still exists in surfing.

WSL has equal pay for top-level competitions. But pay equity does not exist in divisions for younger athletes. For example, at the 2018 Ballito Pro, the two winners of the under-18 division stood side by side. Each of them held a check. Zoë Steyn was the female winner. Her check was

Zoë Steyn surfs in the 2019 World Junior Championships.

worth $4,000. Next to her, the male winner held a check for $8,000. The event's organizers said the boys' prize was larger because more boys had entered the competition.

Although pay inequality continues, conditions are improving for women in surfing. In addition to offering equal pay for the Championship Tour, the WSL announced more opportunities for women to compete. It also said it was working to create more advertising for female surfers. CEWS and WSL are confident that surfing is on the path toward equality.

CHAPTER 6

ARGUING EQUAL PAY

Some of the barriers to equal pay involve leadership. Much of the professional sports world is run by white men. As of 2019, no women were head coaches of a men's professional team. In college sports, women made up only 3 percent of coaches for men's teams. In contrast, white men made up more than 50 percent of all authority positions in both men's and women's sports.

As of 2020, Kristi Toliver was one of the few female assistant coaches in the NBA. The league had no female head coaches.

Opportunities for women have increased over the years. During the 2001–02 NBA season, Lisa Boyer became an assistant coach for the Cleveland Cavaliers. She was the first female assistant coach in the league's history. By the 2019–20 season, the NBA had 11 female assistant coaches. In the NFL, Katie Sowers became an assistant coach for the San Francisco 49ers during the 2019 season. Sowers helped lead the 49ers all the way to the Super Bowl.

Despite these advances, sexism in sports continues. Some examples of sexism are obvious. For instance, women have been shunned or banned from playing sports altogether. During periods when women were not allowed to compete, male athletes dominated the media. Newspapers and TV networks focused on men's sports. Over time, this created a belief that men

⚑ San Francisco 49ers assistant coach Katie Sowers works with players during the 2019 season.

were the default athletes. Patterns of thought, such as who is and isn't an athlete, are difficult for a society to unlearn. As a result, these ways of thinking still influence sports today.

Sexism is easy to identify when a person says women shouldn't play sports. However, sexism is not always so obvious. Sometimes it can be much more subtle. For instance, many people make the claim that women's sports are boring to watch. Even people who have never seen a women's game sometimes hold this opinion. These people may not think their attitudes are sexist. But such beliefs stem from a larger culture of sexism.

Small gestures, such as saying women's sports are boring, can have far-reaching effects. Women's sports receive far fewer endorsements than men's sports. They also receive less media coverage. For example, as of 2019, major sports websites dedicated only 2 to 4 percent of their coverage to women's sports.

Part of this **disparity** is due to a belief that people don't like women's sports. If websites and

▲ Change is unlikely to occur unless news outlets cover more women's sports.

TV networks cover fewer women's games, fewer people watch them. A cycle forms. Fewer viewers can lead to even less coverage. Less coverage means fewer endorsements. When that happens, female athletes struggle to earn higher pay.

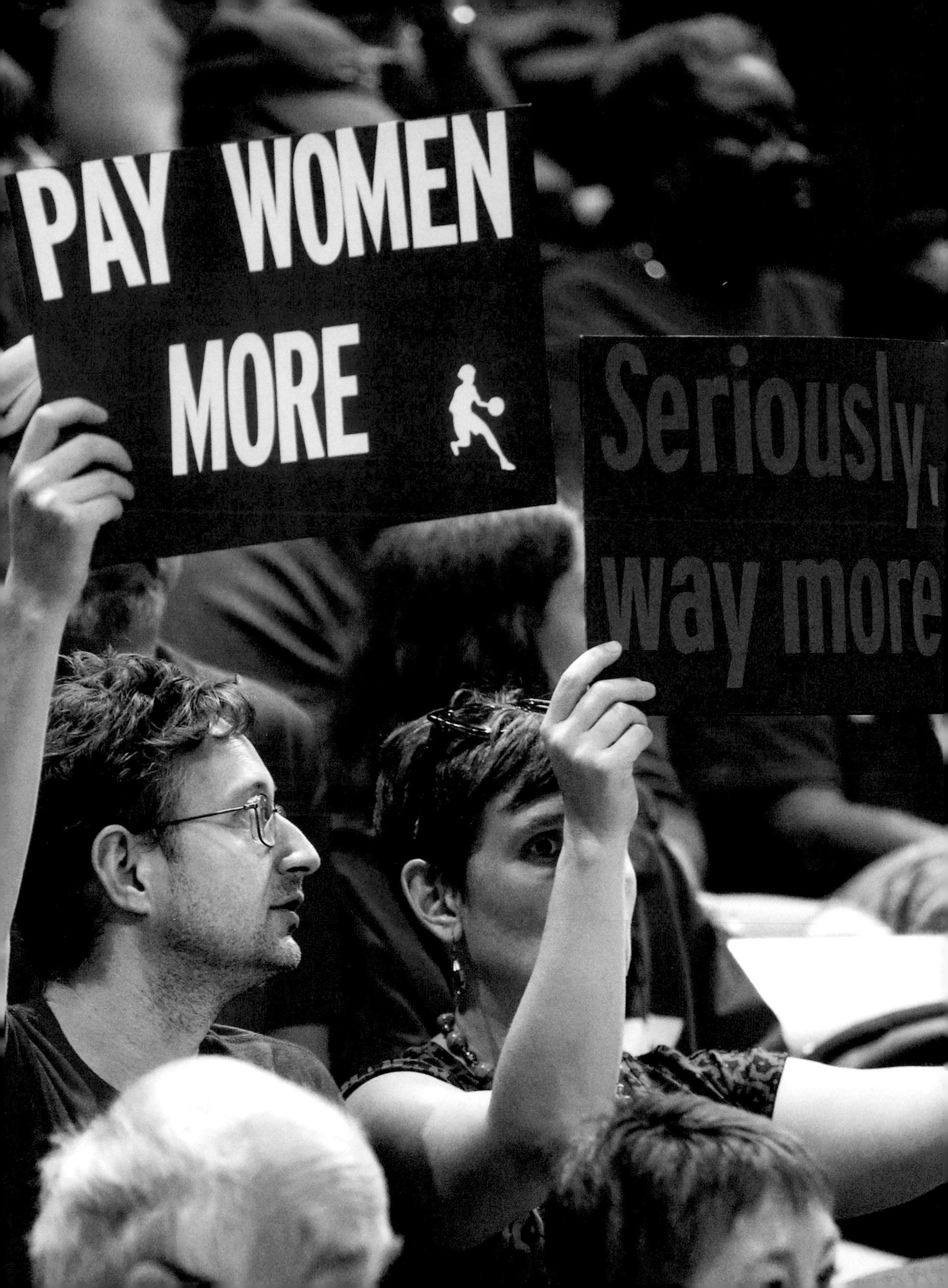
PAY WOMEN MORE
Seriously, way more

CHAPTER 7

EQUAL PAY IN THE FUTURE

Very few professional sports in the United States have equal or even fair pay for women. Several leagues and organizations are working to improve salaries and prize money for female athletes. Even so, most equity occurs only at the highest level of competition. There is still a long way to go in the United States.

Some fair-pay supporters believe that female athletes should strike or boycott their leagues.

Fans speak out at a WNBA game in 2019.

They say these actions could force leagues to make changes. Indeed, some athletes have chosen to strike. However, change is slow and often involves **compromise**. Players get something, but they often have to give up a portion of their demands in order to make progress.

Male athletes also have an important role to play in pay equity. Sexism is a big contributor to the wage gap in professional sports. One of the most effective ways to shift sexist thinking is to have men take a stand. In particular, male athletes can be advocates of women's sports. Male athletes are role models to millions of people. These athletes can use their fame to increase excitement for women's sports.

Fans can help, too. They can support their favorite female athletes. As more people watch games and buy **merchandise**, teams receive more

▲ The Women's US National Hockey Team still faced challenges even after making progress on contracts.

revenue. It will take time. But many sports fans are hopeful that female athletes will achieve pay equity in the future.

PRO ATHLETE PAY EQUITY

Write your answers on a separate piece of paper.

1. Write a paragraph that summarizes the main ideas of Chapter 4.

2. How do you think professional sports would be different if male and female athletes were paid equally?

3. When did Title IX become law in the United States?

    A. 1947

    B. 1972

    C. 2007

4. How does buying a shirt of a women's team help female athletes?

    A. The shirt advertises the team to other people.

    B. The money goes directly to the players on the team.

    C. The shirt company makes more money.

Answer key on page 48.

GLOSSARY

advocates
People who support a specific idea.

boycott
To refuse to participate as a form of protest.

commercial
Having to do with business and making money.

commission
A group working toward a goal.

compromise
An agreement in which both sides give up something they want.

discrimination
Unfair treatment of others based on who they are or how they look.

disparity
A difference or lack of equality.

endorsement
The act of publicly supporting or speaking in favor of a product.

investment
The act of putting money toward something to help it succeed.

merchandise
Manufactured goods that are bought and sold.

promoted
Spoke in favor of something, often in exchange for money.

segregated
Separate or set apart based on race, gender, or religion.

TO LEARN MORE

BOOKS

Harris, Duchess, and Heidi Deal. *Male Privilege.*
Minneapolis: Abdo Publishing, 2018.
Higgins, Melissa, and Michael Regan. *The Gender Wage
Gap.* Minneapolis: Abdo Publishing, 2016.
Ignotofsky, Rachel. *Women in Sports: 50 Fearless Athletes
Who Played to Win.* Berkeley, CA: Ten Speed Press, 2017.

NOTE TO EDUCATORS

Visit **www.focusreaders.com** to find lesson plans,
activities, links, and other resources related to this title.

INDEX

Answer Key: 1. Answers will vary; 2. Answers will vary; 3. B; 4. A